Journal for Women

100 Pages of lightly ruled pages for journaling
and diary entries.

A Notebook for Inspirational
Thoughts and Writings

ISBN 13:978-1541203549
ISBN 10:1541203542

RWSquaredMedia.Wordpress.com

I Can and I Will

I Can and I Will

I Can and I Will

I Can and I Will

I Can and I Will

I Can and I Will

I Can and I Will

I Can and I Will

I Can and I Will

I Can and I Will

I Can and I Will

I Can and I Will

I Can and I Will

I Can and I Will

I Can and I Will

I Can and I Will

I Can and I Will

I Can and I Will

I Can and I Will

I Can and I Will

I Can and I Will

I Can and I Will

I Can and I Will

I Can and I Will

I Can and I Will

I Can and I Will

I Can and I Will

I Can and I Will

I Can and I Will

I Can and I Will

I Can and I Will

I Can and I Will

I Can and I Will

I Can and I Will

I Can and I Will

I Can and I Will

I Can and I Will

I Can and I Will

I Can and I Will

I Can and I Will

I Can and I Will

I Can and I Will

I Can and I Will

I Can and I Will

I Can and I Will

I Can and I Will

I Can and I Will

I Can and I Will

I Can and I Will

I Can and I Will

I Can and I Will

I Can and I Will

I Can and I Will

I Can and I Will

I Can and I Will

I Can and I Will

I Can and I Will

I Can and I Will

I Can and I Will

I Can and I Will

I Can and I Will

I Can and I Will

I Can and I Will

I Can and I Will

I Can and I Will

I Can and I Will

I Can and I Will

I Can and I Will

I Can and I Will

I Can and I Will

I Can and I Will

I Can and I Will

I Can and I Will

I Can and I Will

I Can and I Will

I Can and I Will

I Can and I Will

I Can and I Will

I Can and I Will

I Can and I Will

I Can and I Will

I Can and I Will

I Can and I Will

I Can and I Will

I Can and I Will

I Can and I Will

I Can and I Will

I Can and I Will

I Can and I Will

I Can and I Will

I Can and I Will

I Can and I Will

I Can and I Will

I Can and I Will

I Can and I Will

I Can and I Will

I Can and I Will

I Can and I Will

I Can and I Will

I Can and I Will

I Can and I Will

I Can and I Will

For more amazing journals and adult coloring books from RW Squared Media visit:

Amazon.com
CreateSpace.com
RWSquaredMedia.Wordpress.com

She Believed She Could
So She Did Adult Coloring Book

Life Isn't About Waiting for the
Storm to Pass, It's About Learning
to Dance in the Rain

The Matryoshka Nesting Doll
Coloring Book for Adults

Wine , Cheese, Crackers, and
Coloring

Made in the USA
San Bernardino, CA
31 July 2017